Our purpose at Howard Books is to:
- *Increase faith* in the hearts of growing Christians
- *Inspire holiness* in the lives of believers
- *Instill hope* in the hearts of struggling people everywhere

Because He's coming again!

HOWARD
BOOKS

Published by Howard Books, a division of Simon & Schuster, Inc.
1230 Avenue of the Americas, New York, NY 10020
www.howardpublishing.com

Grandmother: Another Name for Love © 2008 by Alice Gray and Susan Wales

Library of Congress Cataloging-in-Publication Data

Gray, Alice.
Grandmother, another name for love : celebrating the special bond between a grandmother and a grandchild / Alice Gray and Susan Wales.
    p. cm.
1. Grandmothers—Religious life. 2. Grandparent and child—Religious aspects—Christianity. 3. Children—Religious life. I. Wales, Susan. II. Title.
 BV4847.G73 2008
 242'.6431—dc22
 2008015961

ISBN-13: 978-1-4165-6759-2
ISBN-10:   1-4165-6759-3

10 9 8 7 6 5 4 3 2 1

HOWARD and colophon are registered trademarks of Simon & Schuster, Inc.

Manufactured in the United States of America

For information regarding special discounts for bulk purchases, please contact
Simon & Schuster Special Sales at 1-800-456-6798 or business@simonandschuster.com.

Project editor, Chrys Howard
Edited by Between the Lines
Cover design by John Lucas
Interior design by Tennille Paden

With love to my grandchildren,
Breanah Shantel, Summer Malu,
and Cameron Richard

Alice Gray

With love to my granddaughter,
Hailey Elizabeth

Susan Wales

Being a grandmother is like falling in love—
if you haven't experienced it,
you can't imagine how wonderful it feels!

Diane Van Wyk

Contents

Every child born into the world
is a new thought of God,
an ever-fresh and radiant possibility.

Kate Douglas Wiggin

Preface

*Grandchildren are the dots that connect the lines
from generation to generation.*

Lois Wyse

Whether you are a brand-new grandmother or a great-great-grandmother, we want to honor and celebrate the special bond you share with your grandchildren. As you turn these pages, you'll discover endearing stories, gentle wisdom, charming quotes, uplifting scriptures, memorable traditions, tasty recipes, and creative fun—all the things dear to a grandmother's heart . . . and all things you can share with your precious grandchildren.

We hope this inspiring book will not only warm your heart but also become a treasured keepsake for the little ones you love.

A CHILD IS BORN ONLY ONCE,

BUT A GRANDMOTHER IS BORN WITH EACH NEW GRANDCHILD.

Chapter One

A Grandmother Is Born

Daydreams

It's a moment like no other when you first hear those magical words: *You're going to be a grandmother!* Daydreams of tender times to come suddenly dance through your head. You imagine yourself hand in hand with a grandson, the two of you meandering along the seashore, occasionally stopping to wiggle your toes in a gentle wave or to pluck a shell from the sand. Your eyes light up as you envision a tea party with a granddaughter attired in a confection of linen and lace, seated at a table piled high with silver trays of crumpets and scones along with crystal pots of marmalade. The two of you hold out your pinkies and sip mango tea from dainty china cups as this little girl looks up at you with wondrous eyes and smiles.

Then the precious baby is born. You hold the dear one in your arms and gently trace a tiny rosebud mouth with your finger. The daydreams disappear . . . and your real life together as grandmother and grandchild begins.

What's a Gaga?

Susan Wales

*If your baby is beautiful and perfect, never cries
or fusses, sleeps on schedule and burps on demand,
an angel all the time, you're the grandma.*

Teresa Bloomingdale

When my daughter Megan announced that I was about to be a grandmother, one of my first thoughts was, *What will the little cherub call me?* Devouring every grandmother book in sight, I looked here, there, and yonder to read that a particular journalist's mother was called Muv, combining mother and love, and that glamorous actress Goldie Hawn was dubbed Glam-ma. But none of these names suited me, so I sent out an e-mail alert. Replies shot back from all over the world suggesting unique and adorable names—Honey, Peaches, MayMay, Sugar, Grandy, Mugsy, and GiGi, to name a few. Not a one tickled my fancy. What's a grandmother-to-be to do?

This was a job for the Good Mother's Club, a group of friends with whom

I'd met regularly to solve the world's problems back in the day when our kids were at home. Gathered around the luncheon table, my girlfriends offered their suggestions.

"How about Big Mama?" a size-two friend dared to ask. "Remember Big Mama from Tennessee Williams' play, *Cat on a Hot Tin Roof*? You're so Southern. It's the perfect name for you!"

This pleasantly plump grandmother-to-be was not amused. Fortunately, another friend was quick with an alternative: "Don't you think it's darling when a child mixes your name with a grandmother name like Granny Annie? How about Grand-Sue?"

Fabulous, but it wasn't my name, and I deplored being referred to as Sue . . . even by the world's most perfect grandchild. And Grand-Susan was too much of a mouthful for my grandbaby.

"MaMere? Grand-Mere? Mimi?" my Francophile friend suggested in her perfect French accent.

"Now you're talking," I grinned as only an expectant grandmother can. My great-grandmother had a French surname: didn't a trickle of French blood in my veins entitle me to a French name? My own mother is called Mimi by her grandkids, so that was out, and we decided Ma-Mere was a little too superchic for me. But Grand-Mere . . . now, that was the perfect grandmother name for me! I couldn't wait to hear it for the first time from my grandbaby's lips.

Then little Hailey was born and captivated my heart as I'd never imagined anyone or anything could. From the moment I met her, I referred to myself as Grand-Mere. But my darling granddaughter, it turned out, had other ideas. The first grandmother word out of those perfect, bow-shaped lips was "Am-Mommy."

Kinda cute, don't you think? Except the poor child stuttered every time she tried to say Gram-Mommy—"am-am-am-Am-Mommy"—and I longed to make it easier for her.

Even so, I became Am-Mommy, at least for a while. Then one day, after a few stutters, my wonderful little Hailey rolled her big green eyes at me, cocked her head of chestnut ringlets, and exclaimed, "Oh, GaGa!"

And with that my official grandmother name was born at last—GaGa! Not exactly the moniker I'd dreamed of. But no matter. As far as I'm concerned, the little angel can call me anything she pleases—even Big Mama.

Surprisingly, the name GaGa has lived on, even surviving a few bumps along the way, like the time Hailey introduced me to her preschool class.

"Sounds like a bunch of baby talk to me," one of her classmates taunted her.

"What's a GaGa?" another little boy asked.

"A GaGa? It's just anudder mudder who loves me."

Grandmother Is Another Name for Love

*A*lthough *grandmother* is one of the most beautiful words ever spoken, the name your grandchildren call you will always sound like *love*.

Grandmother Names

Bamma	Grandmom	Mo-Mo
BeBe	Grandmomma	Mumsie
BooBaa	Grandnan	Mun
Bubbie	Honey	Muzzy

Gam	LaLa	Namma
GamMa	Lovey	Nana
Goody	Mama Two	Nannie
Gram-Grams	Mamoo	Niny
Gramio	Marmee	Nona
Gramma	Mazoo	Sunny
Grammie	Meemaw	Tootsie
Gramsy	Meez	Tu-Tu
Grand-Bunny	Me-Mah	Two Mama
Grandcracker	Memere	Vo-Vo
Grand-Dear	Mimi	YaYa

Grandmother and Grandfather Names

Bee and Bop	Grandy and Dandy	Mopsy and Popsy
G-Ma and G-Pa	Gummah and Gumpah	Muv and Duv
Go-Go and Po-Po	Mamoo and Papoo	Nonny and Poppy
Goo and Goose	Mop-Mop and Pop-Pop	Oma and Opa

It's such a grand thing to be a mother of a mother—
that's why the world calls her grandmother.

Author Unknown

Dear Heart

Carolyn J. Booth and Mindy B. Henderson
From Grandmother by Another Name

My mother and I were always very close. She was at the hospital when I delivered her first grandchild. After everything was calm, she came in to spend a few minutes with me and her new granddaughter. We huddled close together and stared down at the baby. A rush of emotions flooded through her. She said that it didn't seem so long ago that she had held me just this way upon my birth.

"I want her to call me Dear Heart," she told me.

"Why, Mom?" I asked.

"Because she is the dearest thing to my heart," she replied.

She had other grandchildren after that and felt the exact same way about them. I remember her rocking them and saying, "You are just the dearest thing to my heart."

As the years passed, those children came to understand exactly what their grandmother felt—because they had that same kind of love for her.

Show and Tell

Lois Wyse

From Funny, You Don't Look Like a Grandmother

My very favorite naming story is about Ed and Ethel, who were called the Jewish names "Zaide" and "Bubbie" by their grandson Josh.

When Josh went to nursery school, he talked continually about his zaide and bubbie. He told of adventures with them, and when show and tell day came, he announced that he would bring in his bubbie and zaide.

When he walked in with Ed and Ethel, his nursery school teacher said, "Who are these people?"

"Bubbie and Zaide," he said proudly.

"But . . . but," she stammered, "I thought they were gerbils."

Toddler Spoken Here

Out of the mouth of babes . . .

Psalm 8:2

One of the distinctive joys of grandmothering is the opportunity to relearn that wonderful language called Toddler-Speak. This isn't the same as a baby's sweet jibber-jabber. Oh, not at all. It's a precious language based on the tendency of little ones to coin their own new words and phrases.

Some of these linguistic gems are obvious and easily understood—like *puter* for *computer, hambuggers* for *hamburgers,* and *calerpittar* for *caterpillar.* Others are more creative. For instance, one little granddaughter calls the ice-cream man the Bunny Man because his truck plays the same song as her windup toy bunny. A little boy calls his grandmother BeBack because when she leaves she always promises that she'll be back.

Toddler-Speak is delightful and easy to learn—all you need is a smiling heart.

flutter-by = butterfly

go-go-cycles = motorcycles

pajama shoes = slippers

hello-o-phone = telephone

house truck = motor home

smarshsmallas = marshmallows

rainbrella = umbrella

Walzin' Dizzy = Walt Disney

alligator = escalator

round-and-round = merry-go-round

snacksticks = gymnastics

wet chocolate = chocolate syrup

gigpens = pigeons

tomato = tornado

The Apostles

"So what did you learn in Sunday school?" Tommy's grandmother asked her four-year-old grandson.

"You know those guys that followed Jesus? Well, they're called the twelve opossums."

Welcoming a New Grandchild

The moment I hear a new grandchild is expected, I go in search of quilting fabrics and a pattern to start a keepsake quilt. When the quilt is finished, I include a letter celebrating the day of birth that describes how I felt when I first held the little one in my arms. One day I hope my grandchildren will know that the stitches and the words are keepsakes from my heart.

DIANE VAN WYK

For two hundred years, every grandchild in our family has been christened in an heirloom gown from Sweden. The names and birthdates of all the babies who have worn it are embroidered on the gown.

MARY ELLEN HANSEN

Whenever a grandchild is born, I ask family and close friends to write a contribution for a Shower of Blessings Ceremony. Each participant kneels before the parents, places a hand on the baby, and reads his or her blessing.

Afterward, we circle around the baby's family and pray for God's blessing on them. The written blessings and photos are assembled together into a book and presented to the new parents.

KAREN ROBBINS

I plant a rosebush in my garden to commemorate the arrival of each grandchild. As the children grow, I love to delight them with nosegays and potpourri from "their" bush. When a grandchild marries, I collect the petals from his or her rosebush to be strewn down the aisle.

GRANDMOTHER BENEFIELD

A traditional Austrian baby gift is a candle—to be lit at the christening and on each subsequent birthday until the child is grown and married. The bride and groom then light the candle together at the wedding to symbolize becoming one.

MARGARET "MOCK-MOCK" WESTERMAN

On the day a grandchild is born, I give him or her an add-a-pearl necklace with three pearls, signifying faith, hope, and love. Every birthday or special occasion, I add a pearl to the necklace. When my grandchildren marry, I give them their necklaces—for the girls to wear and for the boys to present to their brides.

MIMI HUEY

It is remarkable how, overnight, a quiet mature lady can learn to sit cross-legged on the floor and play a tin drum, quack like a duck, sing all the verses of "The Twelve Days of Christmas," make paper flowers, draw pigs and sew on the ears of severely-injured teddy bears.

Marlene Walkington Ferber

Dinner Out

Maryann Lee Jacob

We went to a little cafe
just off the campus
to have a quiet dinner together,
the college students there
eating, discussing deep philosophical issues.

You sat at our table
looking suave and debonair in jeans and turtleneck,
your tousled hair shining,
your eyes sparkling, full of mischief.
And you worked your charms
on me and everyone around.

The waitress doted on you,
your cup always filled.
"An extra napkin? Certainly!"
"More crackers for your soup? Of course!"
You flirted notoriously with her
and with the hostess as well,
flashing seductive grins at them,
inviting them to talk,
eating only the fringes of your meal.

Twice you left our table
to walk around
and spread your charms elsewhere,
stopping at a table or two,
grinning broadly, flirtatiously,
soliciting conversation.

I watched you captivate their hearts
and knew you had taken mine,
as I sat quietly observing.

Finally, folding my dinner napkin patiently
and placing it beside my finished plate,
I knew it was time to go,
and walking up to you I said,
"Let's say good-bye."

And picking you up, I placed you
in your stroller,
and as we left,
you waved profusely at everyone,
after your first dinner out with Grandma,
when you were only two.

Tender Moments

*W*ondering what to do with the wedding dress in the attic? These inspiring ideas suggest ways to turn your gown into a treasured family keepsake.

A Baby Pillow

*U*sing the satin from my mother's wedding gown, I made baby pillows for my grandchildren. In the center of each pillow, I stitched a tiny lace pocket for love notes. When my grandchildren married, their ring bearers carried the baby pillows with the wedding rings tucked inside the pockets. The grandchildren are grown now, but they still have their pillows, and I'm still tucking love notes in the pockets.

GRANDMOTHER HUEY

A Bride Doll

I saved my wedding gown for my daughter, but when she married, she wanted her own. Later, when my granddaughters arrived, I bought dolls for them and had a seamstress create bridal gowns for the dolls using the fabric from my wedding dress. The girls are delighted with their bride dolls dressed in Grandma's wedding gown!

SHIRLEY ROSE

Tissue paper flying, my wedding gown soon puddles
about our granddaughter's ankles. A pudgy hand wiggles
out of the satin sleeve to snatch a pink rose from its vase.
The wee one grabs her teddy bear for a bridegroom.
As Bop and I hum the Wedding March, we wonder,
"Was our wedding day as blissful as this moment?"

Author Unknown

GRANDMA ALWAYS MADE YOU FEEL

SHE HAD BEEN WAITING TO SEE JUST YOU ALL DAY

AND NOW THE DAY WAS COMPLETE.

Marcy DeMaree

Chapter Two

Fun at Grandmother's House

Nana's Secret Spice

Adapted from the story "Martha's Secret Ingredient" by Roy J. Reiman

Nana's little granddaughter was curious about the old, dented spice tin Nana kept in the cupboard next to the stove. The small red container with a gold design was faded, worn by time and use. The little girl knew it had to be special, because every time Nana cooked something, she'd sprinkle a little bit of her secret ingredient into the food.

"What's inside there?" the girl would always ask. Nana's blue eyes would twinkle, crinkling at the corners as she smiled to explain. "A secret ingredient—something my mother, grandmother, and even my great-grandmother used in their recipes too. And when you grow up, I'll give you some of my secret ingredient to use when you cook for your family."

When her granddaughter married, Nana presented her with two keepsake gifts—a wooden recipe box filled with family recipes and the faded tin container. The young woman could hardly wait to peek inside the old spice tin! Carefully removing the lid, she was amazed to see that the container was empty—except for a tiny slip of paper frayed and yellowed with age. Passed down through the generations, it was the same slip of paper Nana had received as a young bride from her grandmother.

As the granddaughter read the paper, she could hardly keep back the tears. Written in soft feminine handwriting, the words simply stated: "To everything you make, add a sprinkle of love."

If God had intended us to follow recipes,
He wouldn't have given us grandmothers.

Linda Henley

Someone's in the Kitchen with Nana

Grandmothers never run out of hugs or cookies.
Author Unknown

Soup simmering on the stove, a spoonful of coffee in warm milk, the aroma of apple pie in the oven, kneading bread dough, warm cookies served with milk, pulling a wishbone or licking spoons—all memories of a grandmother's kitchen. It's a magical place where dreams are born and creativity abounds.

Nana's Recipe for Success in the Kitchen

- Illustrate recipe cards for your grandchildren, using pictures from magazines or drawing simple items such as an egg.
- Give each child a recipe box to collect and store his or her favorite recipes. For a special craft, let your grandkids decorate their boxes.

- Provide each child with an apron and a set of tools just for him or her—a wooden spoon and a set of measuring spoons and cups.
- Make place mats that illustrate where the plates, glasses, silverware, and napkins go. On the place mats, write blessings for the children to learn.
- Spark your grandchildren's creativity by providing a variety of items to use for centerpieces. Give them different colors and designs of napkins and plates to select from to set the table.
- Help your grandchildren plan a dinner party for their parents. Create invitations and a centerpiece, plan the menu, cook the food, set the table, and serve Mom and Dad.

Goodies to Cook with the Grandkids

Little Piggies

Watch the movie *Babe* or read *Charlotte's Web*. Afterward, help your grandkids make these yummy Little Piggies:

- 8 hot dogs cut in half
- 8 refrigerator biscuits, uncooked
- 8 slices of cheese, cut in half

*D*ot hot dog halves with mustard and ketchup and wrap in cheese. Cover hot dog with the biscuit dough, sealing at the ends. Cook as directed on the biscuit can and serve.

Ultimate Ice Cream Sandwiches

*C*ombine two of your grandchildren's favorite treats for a scrumptious dessert:

- 1 18-ounce package refrigerated cookie dough
- 3 cups vanilla or chocolate ice cream, slightly softened
- 1 12-ounce package Nestlé Toll House Semi-Sweet Chocolate Mini Morsels

*P*repare cookies according to the package directions. When cool, place 1/2 cup of ice cream on the flat side of a cookie. Top with the flat side of another cookie to make a sandwich. Roll the sides of the ice cream sandwiches in the morsels, and wrap individually in plastic wrap. Store the sandwiches in the freezer for at least one hour prior to serving.

Mimi's Cupcake Cones

Easy for grandkids to make, cupcake cones bring smiles on birthdays and other celebrations.

- 1 cake mix (Betty Crocker Party Rainbow Chip Cake Mix is festive) and accompanying ingredients as listed on box
- 2 12-cup (full-size) muffin pans
- 24 flat-bottom plain or colored ice cream cones
- 1 16-ounce package of ready-made frosting

Preheat oven to 350 degrees. Use cupcake recipe on box as directed, except fill each cone ⅔ full of batter. Place upright in muffin tin to bake. Bake 15 minutes or when toothpick comes out clean. Cool. Frost the cone cakes and serve with a slice of ice cream.

Beach Sandwiches

Chase away the doldrums on a rainy afternoon with a make-believe day at the beach. Give each child a slice of bread with the crusts cut off and a small dish of softened cream cheese that has been tinted blue with food coloring. Help your grandchildren spread the blue cream cheese on the bread with a wooden stick. Decorate the "ocean" using Goldfish crackers and a graham-cracker teddy bear. Slide a gummy ring over the bear for an inner tube. Add a sliced pimento-stuffed olive or a cherry tomato for a beach ball.

No-Bake Peanut Butter Balls

Invite your grandkids to a backyard picnic, and ask them to bring their teddy bears as guests. Help the grandchildren make these tasty treats to share with the bears. For more fun teddy-bear picnic ideas, see our book *Keepsakes for a Mother's Heart*.

- ½ cup peanut butter
- ½ cup honey (Read warnings on honey label)
- 1 cup Rice Krispies
- 2 tablespoons powdered milk

Mix together honey, peanut butter, and powdered milk. Roll into balls, then roll in Rice Krispies.

Popcorn Cake

For special occasions, make a popcorn cake with your older grandkids. They'll enjoy munching this crunchy treat.

- 4 quarts plain, popped popcorn, without salt or butter
- ½ cup vegetable oil
- 1 pound M&M'S Peanut Chocolate Candies
- 1 pound plain or colored marshmallows
- ½ pound salted peanuts
- 1 stick butter

In a large bowl, combine popcorn, M&M's, and peanuts. In a saucepan, melt butter, oil, and marshmallows. Pour over popcorn mix. Press into a buttered tube or Bundt pan. Cool for 30 minutes in refrigerator. Prior to serving, invert on a tray. Cut into wedges. Serves 12.

Keepsake Cookbook

Compile a cookbook for each grandchild with family recipes and traditions. Take photos of you and your grandkids cooking, and include these in the cookbook. Grandmother Sally Knower says she also includes a family tree with a short biography and a photo of the family member from whom the recipe came. Give copies of the cookbook to everyone in the family. What a lovely treasure!

Grand-Mommy's Fun Recipes

Ladybug

To make ladybug, core and halve an apple, and place the flat sides down on a plate. Dot the apple halves with peanut butter, and stick raisins to the dots to make the ladybug's spots.

Banana Dogs

Kids love banana dogs! Spread peanut butter inside a whole-wheat hot dog bun, and place a banana in it. Squirt strawberry jelly from a squeeze bottle for "ketchup." Sprinkle with raisins. How 'bout them yummy dogs!

Creepy Crawlers

Make a creepy crawler. Stack two chocolate sandwich cookies and "glue" together with chocolate frosting. Break bow-tie pretzels apart to make eight curved spider legs. Stick pretzels into the chocolate frosting around the middle of the spider. With frosting, attach two M&M's candies to the front of the cookie stack for eyes.

Grandmas are moms with lots of frosting.

Author Unknown

Mama's Miracles

Jan Karon
From Mitford Cookbook and Kitchen Reader

Editor's note: Jan Karon uses two names for her grandmother—Mama and Miss Fannie.

My grandmother, Miss Fannie, had a miraculous skill: she could make something out of absolutely nothing.

Over and over, she would put a full meal on the table when it didn't appear to my little sister and me that we had anything at all to eat!

Mama's something-out-of-nothing meals might go like this:

First, she'd go out in the yard and catch a chicken. Try doing this; it is *not* easy. After she caught it, she would chop its head off. This seemed the most natural thing in the world to us, then, though I wouldn't relish seeing it done today. She would douse the chicken in a tub of boiling water to loosen its feathers, pluck it over a newspaper, and singe the fine hairs over an open flame in the kitchen wood stove.

Then she would wash the chicken, cut it up, roll the pieces in flour, add salt and pepper, and drop the whole lot into a large iron skillet sizzling with hot bacon grease. There is no high, medium, or low setting on a wood cook stove; she would have to watch that chicken like a hawk while she carried through with the rest of the dinner, which nearly always included a pan of biscuits.

Once the biscuits were cut out with the mouth of a jelly glass, and rising on her battered bake sheet, she might find a head of cabbage and set to work on a bowl of cole slaw, which became famous in our family for its unique style (short on the mayonnaise, long on the salt and vinegar). Then, since we lived in the country, she could always round up a few potatoes, which she would slice and cook, and mash into a silken cloud with milk and butter (often churned by yours truly). About this time, her hand would reach 'way back in the cabinet behind the wood stove, and she would pull out a jar of jam or apple butter or pickles or succotash. And before you know it, Mama had made a meal fit for a king, out of absolutely nothing, don't you know.

By the way, if you have a grandmother, go call her right now and tell her you love her to pieces.

Grandma's Surprise Box

Keep an old travel trunk or fabric-covered box in a cozy corner. Rotate the contents so your grandchildren are always surprised when they look inside. Whimsical books, puzzles, stickers, wooden trucks, Matchbox cars, a miniature tea set, party hats, a little bag with fresh homemade cookies, hand puppets, a chef hat and cookbook, a kite kit, seeds to plant, an art tablet and colored pencils, clues for a treasure hunt, beads to string, or classic games (like marbles, jacks, pick-up sticks and dominoes)—you never know what you might find tucked inside Grandma's surprise box.

Fun in Gran Gran's Backyard

A happy childhood can't be cured.
Mine'll hang around my neck like a rainbow.

Hortense Calisher

The fragrance of flowers tickles our noses. Neighbors chat over rose-covered fences. Sunny skies offer the perfect setting to gather the grandkids in the backyard to play games of hopscotch, croquet, Frisbee, horseshoes, or badminton. Set up a lemonade stand or organize old-fashioned relays or a water-balloon toss. Spray the grandkids with the hose. For grins, let them turn the hose on you. When the sun goes down, dance together under the stars!

Ice Ball Surprise

Insert small toys or pieces of plastic jewelry into balloons. Fill the balloons with water, knot, and freeze until solid. Before giving to your grandchildren, cut away the balloons. They'll have fun pushing their ice ball around a kiddy pool and watching it melt into something special.

Bike Parade

Weave crepe paper through the spokes of bikes and trikes. Show the grandkids how to attach playing cards to the spokes of a bike so they can clack like a motorcycle as they pedal. Include the youngest grandchildren in the parade by decorating their strollers and wagons with tin pie plates, ribbons, and streamers.

Zany Suitcase Relay

Fill two suitcases with old clothes. Make sure each box has the same number of items: underwear, shoes, trousers, shirts, gloves, and hats. Teams line up at the starting line. The first player on each team races to the suitcase, puts on all the clothes, takes them off again, places them back in the suitcase, and races back to tag the next player. The relay continues with each member of the team. The first team to finish wins!

Ice Cream Social

An old-fashioned ice cream social with homemade ice cream churned in a freezer is always a hit. For an evening affair, hang paper lanterns and twinkling lights from the trees. Arrange a sundae bar with all the trimmings and toppings. Be sure to have cones for the younger grandchildren.

Time to Go Home

Three of our grandkids stayed with us for a couple days while their parents celebrated their anniversary. When their mom and dad picked them up to take them home, one of our little granddaughters said, "Grammy, you're going to have to get your own kids! We live with Mommy and Daddy!"
Karen Ellison

I doubt whether the world holds for anyone a more soul-stirring surprise than the first adventure with ice cream.

Heywood Campbell Broun

Growing Up

Marilyn McAuley

Danny was only three when he and his daddy came to live with us. Every morning we would stand at the door and throw kisses and wave good-bye as Grandpa and Daddy left for their jobs. Then Danny and Grandma would build skyscrapers with building blocks and journey into wonderful places by reading book after book. Later we would walk our country lane out to the highway to get the mail and listen to the wind whisper through the tall fir trees.

After work one evening, Grandpa swung Danny in the air and said, "Let's go get a hamburger." As we drove to town, we sang and talked, and then it grew quiet. Danny was thinking.

He said, "Grandpa has a job, and Daddy has a job, and when I grow up, I'll have a job."

"That's right, Danny," said Grandpa.

After a little more thought, Danny added, "And when Grandma grows up, she'll get a job too."

Holidays at Grandmother's House

Over the river and through the woods
to Grandmother's house we go!
Lydia Maria Child

Holidays at Grandmother's house are often the source of a child's warmest memories. Joining hands around a bountiful table to offer thankful praise connects children to a wealth of rich family traditions. Here's a gathering of wonderful activities to do together at holiday time.

Living Easter Basket

If grandchildren ask why eggs are part of the Easter celebration, explain that eggs are a symbol of life. Many families use them as a reminder that Jesus was raised from death to new life. A Living Easter Basket is another way to signify that Jesus lives. Begin this craft one or two weeks before Easter.

- Cardboard milk carton (half-gallon size)
- Construction paper
- Glue
- Stapler
- Poster board or card stock
- Potting soil
- Rye grass seed
- Spray bottle filled with water
- Plastic wrap

Cut off the top of a milk carton and glue construction paper to the outside. Make a handle with poster board and a stapler. Fill the container with potting soil and sprinkle with grass seed. Mist with a spray bottle and cover with plastic wrap. Sit the "basket" in the sun and mist daily. When the grass sprouts, remove the plastic and continue to mist. By Easter morning, it will be the perfect spot to hide a few colored eggs.

Easter Sleeping Cookies

Celebrate the miracle of Easter with your grandchildren. As you make these "sleeping cookies" together, share the Bible story of Jesus' crucifixion and resurrection. What lasting memories you'll create!

- 1 cup pecan pieces
- 1 Ziploc quart-size bag
- Wooden spoon
- 1 teaspoon vinegar
- Paper cups (one for each child)
- Pinch of salt
- 1 cup sugar
- Plastic spoons (one for each child)
- 3 egg whites
- 1 cup chocolate morsels
- Waxed paper
- Cookie sheet
- Masking tape

Preheat oven to 300 degrees. Follow the story and steps below.

- *After the Roman soldiers arrested Jesus, they beat him.* Place pecan pieces in a Ziploc bag. Have the children beat the nuts with a wooden spoon to break into smaller pieces. Set aside.

- *Jesus grew thirsty on the cross, and the soldiers gave him vinegar to drink.* Fill paper cups with a taste of vinegar for the children to sample. Pour 1 teaspoon of vinegar into a mixing bowl.

- *Salt represents the salty tears cried by the followers of Jesus.* Sprinkle salt into the grandchildren's hands for them to taste. Drop a pinch of salt into the mixing bowl.

- *The sweetest part of the story—because he loves us, Jesus died for us.* Give the children a smidgen of sugar to taste on plastic spoons. Add a cup of sugar to the mixture.

- *Jesus forgives us. He covers our sins and makes us white as snow.* Add egg whites, and beat with an electric mixer for 15 minutes or until they form stiff peaks. Fold the nuts and chocolate chips into the mixture while explaining that when we believe in Jesus, he forgives and covers our sins, just as the egg whites cover the nuts and morsels.

46

- *After Jesus died on the cross, the Roman soldiers sealed his body inside a tomb.* Drop meringue mixture by teaspoon onto a cookie sheet lined with waxed paper. Slide the cookie sheet into the oven, close the door, and turn off the oven. Give each child a piece of masking tape to symbolically seal the oven door.
- *When Jesus' friends left his tomb, they were sad.* Tell the children you understand that they feel sad leaving the cookies in the oven, but tomorrow they can look forward to a great surprise!
- *Christ is risen today!* On Easter morning, gather the children around the oven. Tell them that when Jesus' friends returned to the tomb the next morning, it was empty! An angel told them, "He is not here. He is risen!" Ask the children to pull the tape off the oven door. What a surprise to discover that the meringues have risen into cookies! As the children bite into them, note that these meringues are empty inside, just as the tomb was. Rejoice! Sing an Easter hymn.

Thanksgiving Journal

Purchase a scrapbook or journal for each grandchild, and help him or her decorate it with an autumn motif. Every year, go around the Thanksgiving table and ask family members to tell what they're thankful for. Jot down notes of the blessings, and take lots of family photos. Make decorative copies of the blessings, and place them with the photos inside each grandchild's book. These books will become treasured keepsakes throughout the years.

Christmas Treasure Hunt

Family gatherings at Christmastime provide a precious opportunity to teach your grandchildren about the true meaning of Christmas. To familiarize them with the characters in the Christmas story, why not give grandchildren an unbreakable nativity set? You can even suggest a game like this one, found in our book *A Keepsake Christmas:*

Hide the nativity pieces for a treasure hunt. Add extra angels and shepherds if necessary so that every child can find at least one item. Once all the pieces are found, read the Christmas story from Luke 2:1–20 and Matthew 2:9–11. As each nativity piece is mentioned in the Bible, let the grandchildren place the appropriate figure near the manger.

A Grandmother Tree

Vickie "Nana" Foard

Grandchildren love coming to Nana's house because it's so different from home—full of nooks and corners to explore, hidden treasures to discover, odd-shaped cooking utensils, sweet-smelling sheets, new places for hide-and-seek, favorite books that Mommy and Daddy read when they were little, Raggedy Ann and Andy dolls . . . and most intriguing of all—a Grandmother Tree.

Purchase a small, artificial tree with lots of branches. Spray paint it if you wish. Then fill an attractive container with small stones and "plant" the tree.

At Christmas, decorate the tree with twinkle lights and ornaments. Leave the lights on throughout the year, and change the ornaments to fit the occasion. For birthdays, weave ribbons through the branches and attach photos of the birthday celebrant. Deck the tree out in hearts, flowers, and keepsake valentines in February. Easter calls for crosses, decorative eggs, and toy chicks and bunnies; miniature flags and paper firecrackers are ideal for patriotic days. When it's back-to-school time, hang pencils, rulers, and apples on the tree. Pumpkins, autumn leaves, and gourds are perfect for fall trees. Now, can you believe it's time for Christmas again?

Always Christmas

If you come to my house, you might find it curious to see a nativity scene on the dining room windowsill with every chunky figure crowded atop the roof of the wooden stable. It has sat there for three years. Christopher was almost one when he started carrying a shepherd or donkey in a chubby fist and rearranging the characters in the greatest story ever told. At Grandma's house, it's not always winter, but it's always Christmas.

Patty Duncan

Tender Moments

An Antique Candlestick

Charlotte Adelsperger

On Christmas Eve our three grandchildren come with their parents to our home. I point them to my special keepsake on a table. It's a 140-year-old pewter candlestick that displays a tall red candle.

"I remember this candlestick in my parents' house when I was growing up," I tell them. "My mother would tie a red bow on it at Christmas."

The children know the history. The seven-inch candlestick first belonged to my great-great-grandmother, who lived around the time of Abraham Lincoln. It was passed to each generation, and then to me. Every person who owned it believed that Jesus is the Light of the world.

After a prayer together, we light the candle. It glows and flickers all evening as we celebrate Christ's birth.

51

GRANDPARENTS SORT OF SPRINKLE STARDUST

OVER THE LIVES OF LITTLE CHILDREN.

Chapter Three

Adventures with Grandmother

Adventures with Big Mama

From a book of memories written by Big Mama's granddaughters,
Harriot Hall, Nancy Bradsher, and Susan Wales
Adapted by Susan Wales

When you were a little girl, did you go to your grandmother's house?" my little granddaughter asked me.

I wasn't sure how I was going to explain Big Mama—not your typical grandmother by any stretch of the imagination. Barely tipping the scales at one hundred pounds, Big Mama earned her title by her presence, not her size. At Big Mama's house there were no hugs, bedtime stories, or even cookies. But, oh, there were adventures, so I dared to share one with my granddaughter!

"Big Mama adamantly believed everyone needed a new Sunday go-to-meeting hat at Easter. Rarely did she drive her big black car to town, but on this particular day, Big Daddy had borrowed her chauffeur to drive him way out in the country on a house call to check on a sick patient. Big mistake!

" 'Aren't we lucky ducks,' Big Mama exclaimed to my cousins and me as she pulled into the parking spot right in front of Belk Gallant's Department Store.

It was her favorite expression, but believe me, we weren't so lucky that day. A spider dared creep under the veil of her flowered hat, and the scare caused her foot to slip off the brake. The big black car lunged as it jumped the curb, mowing down a parking meter before crashing through the department store window! Just as it came to rest on two of its wheels, a dark-haired mannequin in a seersucker suit shot through the back window and landed in my lap, its long plastic legs protruding out of the car!

"In a daze, I surveyed the scene. The pink Easter bonnet I'd coveted no longer graced the head of a pretty blonde mannequin; it was twirling about on the car's antenna. A red-faced, arm-waving store manager was already at the window, jumping up and down. 'Turn off the car, Miss Juliabel,' he ordered—sweetly at first. But when Big Mama didn't pay him a lick of attention, his voice grew louder and angrier as he yelled it over and over again.

"Totally ignoring the 'young whippersnapper,' Big Mama turned to us and said, 'Get out of the car!' Before we could move, she had yanked the mannequin, my cousins, and me from the car. By then a crowd had gathered, and a dapper gentleman in a polka-dot bow tie offered us a hand down out of the store window.

"Everyone gasped at what Big Mama did next. With her pocketbook swinging on her arm to the beat of her favorite country tune, 'Hey, good lookin', whatch a got cookin'?—which still blared from the car radio—Big Mama held her head high and paraded us down Main Street toward home as if nothing ever happened!

"As I looked back, I cringed at the sight of Big Mama's huge black car in the shattered store window; its engine still roaring and its wheels still spinning. It was an adventure I'll never forget." I sighed as the story came to an end.

"But ... but what about your pink Easter bonnet?" my granddaughter asked with great concern.

"On Easter Sunday, my cousins and I wore the same old hats to church we'd worn the year before," I explained. "But no one seemed to notice. They were too busy talking about our adventure with Big Mama!"

For a moment my granddaughter just sat there, her eyes wide with amazement. Then she finally asked, "Will you take me on an adventure?"

Lights! Camera! Action!

All the world's a stage.

William Shakespeare

What fun to stage a play, concert, or recital with the grandchildren. Plan your own *American Idol* or karaoke night, and ask the gang to sing along. It's also fun to act out a favorite fairy tale. Stage a pageant at Easter, Thanksgiving, and Christmas. A little imagination, a little planning . . . and everyone can be a star!

- First determine the type of show to produce. Impromptu performances are fun, but more elaborate shows take practice, planning, and preparation.
- Find a spot for your theater—a garage, a basement, or outdoors. Set up chairs for your audience. And don't forget the popcorn!
- Design invitations or playbills on colorful paper using markers, stickers, glitter, sequins, and photos. Have the grandkids choose their stage names for the program.

- Gather clothes and funky accessories to create imaginative costumes.
- Kids adore hair and makeup artistry. Old wigs and hairpieces add a touch of glamour. Streak hair with wild colors using washable sprays from beauty-supply stores. Apply stick-on tattoos or gobs of stage makeup, or try face painting.
- Props add to performances—a manger for a Christmas pageant, a baby doll for Baby Jesus, or staffs for the shepherds. Family pets in costumes make great props too!

Lights! Camera! Action! Shine a spotlight on the performers, and hand them a microphone. Record the play with a camcorder. Throughout the years you'll have loads of fun watching these star performances. And who knows? Maybe one day Hollywood, the pulpit, or a concert hall will call!

Recipe for Face Painting

- 1 heaping teaspoon cornstarch
- ½ teaspoon cold cream
- ½ teaspoon water

- 2 drops food coloring
- Small makeup brush or sponge

Stir together starch and cold cream until well blended. Add water and stir, then add food coloring. Store in an airtight container. Washes off with soap and water.

Apply with brush, sponge, or fingers. Let one layer dry before applying another. Use stencils to make stars, hearts, and flowers. Add glitter for a dramatic effect. Be careful not to get paint or glitter near the eyes.

Imagination! Imagination! I put it first years ago, when I was asked what qualities I thought necessary for success on the stage.

Ellen Terry

Grandmas don't just say, "that's nice"—
they reel back and roll their eyes and throw up their hands
and smile. You get your money's worth out of grandmas.

Pam Brown

Dancing to the Oldies!

Dancing with the feet is one thing, but dancing with the heart is another.

Author Unknown

Catch a little Saturday Night Fever by turning a room or a garage into a disco! Teach the dances you danced as young person, and have the grandkids teach you theirs . . . and don't forget to laugh! This can be one of the most memorable and hilarious evenings ever spent with the grandkids.

A Hoppin' Poppin' Disco Floor

Cover the floor with a roll of packing bubbles from the moving supply store. It's noisy and fun to dance on the bubbles, and what kid doesn't love to pop 'em?

Lighting Up Your Disco

String twinkling lights around the room, hooking them over curtain rods or plants. Hang a mirrored disco ball from the ceiling. Mirrored balls are easy to find in stores at Christmastime, or you and the grandkids can make one by gluing mirrored tiles to a Styrofoam ball. For added excitement, position spotlights at the corners of the room to angle on the disco ball.

Disco Music

Purchase CDs of 1950s, '60s, '70s, and '80s dance music. Ask the grandkids to choose from your collection or to bring some of their own music.

Disco Attire

For fun, wear multiple Lite-Rope necklaces and bracelets (available for purchase at party-supply stores or online).

1950s Style

Wear a circular skirt and bobby socks—no shoes allowed for a '50s sock hop. Cut out poodle felt appliqués to pin or stick on skirts. Gramps and the guys, roll up your jeans and shirt cuffs and slick back your hair.

1960s Style

Choose from bell-bottoms, miniskirts, or maxiskirts, granny dresses, and go-go boots for '60s music. For the perfect '60s accessories, wear granny glasses and floppy hats or flowers in your hair.

1970s Style

Dress up a bit! Dresses, skirts, and platform shoes for the girls. Jumpsuits, tight shirts, and polyester pants with boots for the guys. Wear tropical and bold prints in the brightest of colors.

1980s Style

It's funky time! Wear jeans and white T-shirts with the sleeves rolled up, and don Doc Martens or other heavy boots. Gel the hair, use stick-on tattoos, and wear black leather bracelets.

Dancing the Night Away

Okay everybody, it's time to put on your dancing shoes! Your grandkids will roll with laughter as you demonstrate the twist, the shag, the mashed potato, the jerk, the monkey, the Texas two-step, and the bunny hop. If you can still get down on the floor, don't forget the gator or the crocodile! Include some favorite dances from yesteryear, like the Charleston, the tango, the jitterbug, or the polka. Let your little ones stand on your feet, and waltz them around the room.

Remember to give the grandkids an opportunity to play their music and show you their dances!

When the Music Stops

Stage a contest to see who can stomp the most of the remaining bubble-wrap bubbles. Award trophies or prizes for the best dancer in every possible category so that everybody wins—funniest, silliest, fastest, oldest. Afterward, set up your own soda shop to serve burgers and fries, Coke floats, or milkshakes.

A child sings before he speaks, dances almost before he walks. Music is in our hearts from the beginning.

Pamela Brown

Pirate Treasure Hunt

To find it you must sail to the end of the earth and beyond.

Captain Jack Sparrow

Yo ho ho! Grandchildren of all ages love dressing up like swashbuckling pirates to hunt for treasure! This adventure is a great outdoor activity and the perfect indoor pastime on rainy days. Create an island with fishnets, ropes, seashells, and plastic alligators and fish. Fill a treasure chest with colored beads and "gold" coins. Fly the skull-and-crossbones Jolly Roger flag from a tree or mantel . . . and set sail together!

Treasure Map

Illustrate clues and treasures with drawings, photos, or cutouts from magazines for young pirates who can't read treasure maps. For example, if you hide golden apples behind a tree, draw a picture of a tree and apples. Give each treasure site on the treasure map an adventuresome name, like Shark Pit, Skull Crossing, or Alligator's Nest.

Pirates' Loot

Bird feathers, shells, colored beads, shiny rings, a pirate whistle, stickers, and Goldfish crackers are treasures you can hide. Fill a "treasure chest" with gold foil–wrapped coins, or cover plastic eggs in gold foil and fill with dimes or gummy fish.

Pirate Garb

Press on a skull-and-crossbones temporary tattoo purchased in a toy department, or draw the "tattoo" on arms or cheeks with washable color markers. For less scrubbing later, draw the tattoo on Band-Aids.

Make swashbuckling hats from construction paper, or tie a colorful bandanna around each grandchild's head. For eye patches, cut circles of black felt and attach with elastic. Blacken or yellow teeth with tooth makeup from the costume shop.

A spyglass is fun and simple to make. Provide each child with an empty paper-towel roll to cover in aluminum foil. Stretch clear plastic wrap over one end and secure with tape.

Make miniature pirate ships using half a walnut shell for the hull. Press chewing gum into the shell, and insert a fishing weight into the gum so the boat will float. Assist younger children with a toothpick, then spear a triangular-shaped colored paper for a mast and insert it into the gum.

Pirate Grub

Hot dogs make the perfect pirates' grub. Cut and attach a triangular-shaped piece of iceberg lettuce to a pretzel stick and insert the "sail" into the center of the roasted hot dog. Serve Goldfish crackers and stuffed olives to your one-eyed pirates. "Ants" can walk the plank in celery stuffed with peanut butter and dotted with raisins. And your pirates will love frozen bananas dipped in chocolate for dessert.

Dropping the Anchor

After your treasure hunt, watch an adventure DVD such as *Swiss Family Robinson*. Or read from Robert Louis Stevenson's classic *Treasure Island* or, for toddlers, Kathy Tucker's *Do Pirates Take Baths?*—until it's time to sail away to the next adventure . . . the land of dreams!

Come, cuddle your head on my shoulder, dear,
Your head like the golden-rod,
And we will go sailing away from here
To the beautiful land of Nod.

Ella Wheeler Wilcox

Attic Dance

Robin Jones Gunn

Little Rachel was thrilled to find that Gramma Pat has a "real attic." When she opened one of the large, barrel-top trunks and looked inside, her face lit up the room! You'd have thought she had discovered buried treasure. The trunk brimmed with an assortment of faded, crumpled, fancy dresses. I stood there in the heat and dust, barely able to breathe.

But Rachel was in heaven.

"Where'd you get this one, Gramma Pat?" Rachel asked.

"The blue one? Oh, my. I wore that to the Indian Summer Dance at the lake when I was seventeen."

Rachel pulled out a yellowed gown with a moth-eaten collar made of rabbit fur. Gramma Pat said it was from the Christmas Ball when she was crowned the second runner-up for Snow Princess.

"What about this one?" Rachel extracted a short, black taffeta dance skirt. It had layers of netting that made it stick out. The waistband was torn on the side. It was from some sort of "Nights in Paris" dance revue. Gramma Pat said she lost the magenta bolero that went with it. I felt like muttering, "Oh, too bad."

Bur Rachel was in awe. "It's the most beautiful skirt in the whole world!" she said. She tried it on and we were immediately treated to a lively performance of twirls and curtsies. The skirt hadn't had a workout like that in fifty years.

As we watched Rachel dance, utterly charmed in spite of the new clouds of dust, I told Pat, "I can see now why you kept all this stuff."

She laughed and said, "Oh, that's not why I kept them. I kept them so I'd know it wasn't all a dream."

When she said those words, the years seemed to roll away from her face. Her eyes got all sparkly and dewy. I watched her tuck the snow princess dress back in the trunk, and I felt quite sure that she still has a dream or two spinning in that lovely head of hers.

Do you know what keeps going through my mind? That I'll wake up some morning and these precious moments will seem just like a dream.

But then . . . all I'll really have to do is check Rachel's closet for the frilly taffeta skirt. Yes, Gramma Pat let Rachel take the "most beautiful skirt in the whole world" home with her. One small glimpse and sweet memories dance in my heart.

Tender Moments

What grandmother doesn't cherish recollections of little ones slipping tiny feet into Grammy's grown-up shoes or Grampy's too-big slippers? Create a "Grammy's Dress-Up Box" and welcome your grandchildren into the magical world of make-believe. Whether pretending to be an enchanted princess, a glamorous movie star, or an action hero, children will have hours of fun playing dress-up—and Grandma will have a treasure chest of keepsake memories!

- Paint an old suitcase with your grandchildren's favorite color of acrylic paint. Let the kids decorate it with jewels, glitter, or stickers, and store the dress-up clothes in it.
- Take the grandkids to garage sales and thrift shops and search for costume jewelry, baubles, and trinkets. The glitzier the better.

- Check out hardware stores. Little builders or firemen love inexpensive goggles, gloves, and hard hats, and future doctors like wearing protective face masks.
- Ask friends and relatives to save Halloween costumes and dance outfits when their own children outgrow them.
- Collect scarves, bandannas, boas, ties, shawls, and remnants of fabric—tulle for bridal veils, red or black cotton for hero capes, and bright satin for exotic turbans.
- Dig out prank items you've collected over the years: ties with blinking lights, fake teeth, and crazy hats.
- Buy funky accessories like plastic tiaras, wigs, wands, fans, large plastic sunglasses, handbags, gloves, hats, and sheriff stars.
- Don't forget shoes. Give up some of your out-of-style fancy shoes, as long as the heels aren't too high. Grampy's old boots are perfect for young firemen, carpenters, soldiers, and astronauts.
- Bring out Grammy's Dress-Up Box on a rainy day, and let the fun begin!

Whispers of yesterday and glimmers of tomorrow
All dancing out of Grandma's dress-up box today.

Kimber Annie Engstrom

GRANDMOTHERS HAVE TO ANSWER QUESTIONS LIKE

"WHY ISN'T GOD MARRIED?" AND

"HOW COME DOGS CHASE CATS?"

Bobby, age 8

Chapter Four

GRANDMOTHER'S INSPIRING MOMENTS

Things I've Learned from My Grandchildren

Along the road of grandmothering, there will be a million moments when you inspire your grandchildren. Just as often, seeing the world through their eyes will delight and inspire you. We hope you enjoy this small gathering of ideas and fun observations.

- Playing in a mud puddle is more fun than taking a bubble bath.
- Poems don't have to rhyme.
- Four-year-olds can usually repeat word for word what you shouldn't have said.
- It's more fun to eat peanut butter, raisins, and celery if you call it "Ants on a log."
- Finding a small green worm can be almost as much fun as playing on an expensive swing set.
- If you drop a hard-boiled Easter egg on the floor and it cracks, give it to someone anyway and say, "Look! It's starting to hatch."

- Sometimes we need to be loved the most when we deserve it the least.
- Band-Aids and kisses always make an "owie" feel better.
- Anything can be a toy.
- You'll have a lot more respect for a bird after you try making a nest.
- If you want to see a shooting star, you have to spend a lot of nights looking up.
- A grandmother's lap cures more tears than candy.

New Inspiration for an Old Game

Photograph your grandchildren, their toys, pets, family members, and friends, and make two prints of each. Shuffle the pictures and place them facedown on a table. Take turns turning up two pictures at a time. When you find a match, remove those two pictures. If the photos are different, turn them back over and continue playing until all the pairs are matched.

Only when children gather
is there any real chance of fun.

Mignon McLaughlin

The Magical Hour

Susan Wales

There is more treasure in books than in all the pirates' loot on Treasure Island . . . and best of all, you can enjoy these riches every day of your life.

Walt Disney

My love of reading first began with cherished story hours in my grandmother's rocking chair at her house in the country.

My granddaddy gets a smidgen of the credit because he was always eager to share a spooky tale that made my sister, my cousins, and me all shriek and shrill. And I'll never forget his special treat for story time—a frosty glass filled with chocolate milk and crushed ice.

But it was my grandmother who truly opened the gate to the enchanting kingdom of books. She not only told stories—she added props! If we read *Jack and the Beanstalk*, she would prepare the giant's snack for us—a hunk of bread and a piece of cheese. Then we'd go plant a seed in the garden, hopeful our vine might spring up to take us to a giant's house above the clouds. When we played dress-up in Grandmother's gowns and jewels, sipping sherbet punch while listening to *Cinderella*, her eyes always misted over. Now, as a grandmother myself, I realize she was reminiscing about her younger years, when she'd donned those frocks and attended her own Cinderella balls.

Story time at my grandparents' house was a magical hour filled with moments that fueled our imaginations, carrying us to exotic places around the world and introducing us to intriguing people. And, oh, the lessons we learned. Grandmother regaled us with tales of the olden days that sparked a love of history. Granddaddy's Bible stories instilled in me a lifelong passion for Scripture. *The Little Red Hen* taught us the valuable lesson of "I'll do it myself." *The Little Engine That Could* inspired us to reach for the moon. David and Goliath taught us courage and trust in God. Passages from *Little Women* and *Little House on the Prairie* entertained us while making us mindful of our many blessings.

These magical hours have become a treasured tradition in our family. My mother re-created them for both her children and grandchildren, and today she entertains her great-grandchildren by reading from current children's books as well as the worn, dog-eared volumes from our childhood.

Now I adore re-creating the story hour for my granddaughter Hailey. And I must confess that on occasion she and I get into trouble with her mommy for staying up past bedtime reading book after book. Luckily, my flashlight's tucked beneath the pillow.

Today I glance over at four-year-old Hailey, all dressed up in princess fluff, her curls adorned with a sparkling crown and her toes tucked into glass slippers, and my eyes mist with tears. As we sip pink sherbet punch and read *Cinderella*, I am transported back to a precious time and place in my own childhood where I hear the creak of the antique rocker and remember my grandmother's voice, "Once upon a time . . ."

Reading means time, a lap
to sit on, hands to turn pages and a
voice of love—gifts to a child that last a lifetime.

Francine Rivers

The history of our grandparents is remembered
not with rose petals but in the laughter and tears
of their children and their children's children.

Charles and Ann Morse

A Merry Heart

Does a duck in a cup or a cat in a tutu make you smile?
Your grandchildren think these images are hilarious.

AARP, "Laughing with Your Grandchildren"

Whether it's the first little grin when a baby plays peekaboo or the spontaneous giggles of a second-grader telling a knock-knock joke, laughter can be a special language between you and your grandchildren. Sing a silly song, pretend to be a purple poodle, or wear a funny hat. Go ahead, laugh your hearts out . . . together! And while you're at it, Grandma, enjoy a little chuckle with these cuties.

Cure for the Giggles

Six-year-old Angie and her four-year-old brother Joey were sitting together in church. Joey giggled, sang, and talked out loud. Finally his big sister had had enough.

"You're not supposed to talk out loud in church."

"Why? Who's going to stop me?" Joey asked.

Angie pointed to the back of the church and said, "See those two men standing by the door? They're hushers."

First Pancake

Grandmother was preparing pancakes for her grandsons: Kevin, age five, and Ryan, who was three. When the boys began to argue over who would get the first pancake, their grandmother saw the opportunity for a moral lesson.

"If Jesus were sitting here," she said, "He would say, 'Let my brother have the first pancake. I can wait.'"

Kevin turned to his younger brother and said, "Ryan, you be Jesus."

What Does God Look Like?

A grandmother asked her granddaughter what she was drawing, and the little girl replied, "I'm drawing God."

"But no one knows what God looks like."

Without missing a beat or looking up from her drawing, the girl replied, "They will in a minute."

A Budding Author?

Just a few weeks after her fifth birthday, little Summer Malu burst through the front door and chirped, "Nana, let's write a book. I'll tell you a story about a white horse, and you can type the words on your 'puter. I'll draw the pictures, and we can make a pretty cover with my name on it."

I picked her up and twirled her around. "Oh, Summer, this is the best idea ever!" And so it came to be that Summer Malu has her first "published" work, and Nana has a memorable keepsake.

Alice Gray

Grandmother-grandchild relationships are simple.
Grandmas are short on criticism
and long on love.

Anonymous

Conversations with God

Dear God,

I didn't think orange went with purple until I saw the sunset you made on Tuesday. That was cool!

EUGENE

Dear God,

Did you mean for the giraffe to look like that, or was it an accident?

NORMA

Dear God,

Thank you for my baby brother, but what I prayed for was a puppy.

JOYCE

Dear God,

If you watch me in church Sunday, I'll show you my new shoes.

MICKEY

Dear God,

I think about you sometimes, even when I'm not praying.

ELLIOTT

A joyful heart is good medicine.

Proverbs 17:22 NASB

Five-Fingered Prayer

The moments you spend praying with your grandchildren are never ordinary—they are golden. Here's a simple exercise for teaching little ones how to pray. Help the child place palms together in a traditional prayer position, with thumbs closest to the body. Then show him or her how to use each finger as a prayer reminder:

Your Thumb

Begin by praying for those closest to you . . . your family.

Your Pointing Finger

Next, pray for those who need wisdom in pointing others in the right direction . . . ministers, missionaries, and doctors.

Your Tallest Finger

This reminds us of those God has placed in authority over us . . . our president, parents, teachers, and police officers need God's guidance.

Your Ring Finger

This is our weakest finger. It reminds us to pray for those in need . . . those who are poor, in pain, or in trouble.

Your Little Finger

This is when you pray for your own needs and desires . . . asking the Lord to watch over you and to bless you.

Learned by Heart

The LORD is my shepherd; I shall not want.

Psalm 23:1 KJV

A friend told us a story she had read about a little four-year-old girl who was asked by her Sunday-school teacher if she would like to learn the entire Twenty-third Psalm as a surprise for her parents. Looking at the teacher's kind face, the blue-eyed little girl said, "Oh, I already know that psalm by heart."

"You do?" the teacher asked in surprise.

"Oh, yes, I learned it from my grandmother." Standing up, the girl gave a little bow and said, "The Lord is my shepherd, that's all I want." She bowed again and then sat down.

Blinking back tears, the teacher said, "I think that's the most wonderful way I've ever heard that psalm."

Tender Moments

*S*imply cherishing your grandchildren can inspire them to greatness!

This truth is often heard in the words of an acceptance speech for an Oscar or a Nobel Prize, or in a president's inaugural address. A grandmother's influence can be found in best sellers, scientific discoveries, medical breakthroughs, winning games, or designs in art or fashion—all inspired by somebody's grandmother.

- An artist who discovered that his grandmother had tucked away his art in her dresser drawer found the courage to pursue a career in his lifelong passion.
- A world-renowned author said her grandmother was the inspiration for the lead character in her famous mysteries.

- Many pastors attribute their ministries to the faithful prayers of a grandmother.

Treasured keepsakes in a drawer, whispered prayers, and tender words of encouragement—these inspire dreams in the lives of your grandchildren!

The reason God made grandmas
is they are sweet, they comfort you when you're sad,
and most of all, they love you.

Breanah, age 8

My grandmother would say, "Make sure you look good. Make sure you speak well. Make sure you remain that Southern gentleman that I've taught you to be."

Jamie Foxx

SHE IS THE ONE PERSON IN THE WORLD

WHO LOVES YOU WITH ALL HER HEART,

WHO REMEMBERS THE CHILD YOU WERE

AND CHERISHES THE PERSON YOU'VE BECOME.

Barbara Cage

Love Is a Grandmother

Legacy of Love

Alice Gray

I am delighting in this wonderful season of being a grandmother. Once again I'm making cardboard forts in our living room and walking hand-in-small-hand on a starlit night to find the Milky Way. Storybooks put away for years are read again, almost by heart, from well-worn pages. I lift little ones up onto painted carousel horses and feel the air softly ruffle my hair as we ride round and round. No matter how old my grandchildren grow, I still call them Precious, soothe their bumped knees, and give encouragement when their way seems hard.

At bedtime I give good-night kisses and say quiet bedtime prayers. I cup little faces in my hands and ask, "Who loves you?"

A smile spreads across rosy cheeks. "Grandma loves me," a soft voice answers, "and Mommy and Daddy and God."

Whispering a nighttime blessing, I tuck Brown Bear or White Horse under the covers. Then, as I turn to dim the lights, I hear, "Grandma, I love you." A tear slips down my cheek, and the legacy of love continues.

A Grandmother's Prayer

Dear one . . .
May the LORD bless you
and protect you.
May the LORD smile on you
and be gracious to you.
May the LORD show you his favor
and give you his peace.

Numbers 6:24–26 NLT

*If you have knowledge,
let others light their candles in it.*

Margaret Fuller

Ways to Love Your Grandchildren

*I know my grandma loves me 'cause when I look into
her eyes, I can see all the way to her heart.*

From a seven-year-old

You can't say the words "I love you" too often. But along with your words,
here are a few ideas that will make your grandchildren feel treasured.

- Turn off the electric lights and color together by candlelight.
- Write your grandchildren letters telling how much you value them.
  Point out their good qualities, and encourage them in their goals.
- Freeze Beanie Babies to use to soothe owies.
- Buy a heart-shaped stepping-stone for the backyard. Write your grand-
  children's names on the stone with enamel paint. On the back, write
  each one's date of birth and a prayer.

- Help your grandkids understand how much God treasures them by reading them Bible stories and taking them to Sunday school and church whenever they visit you for the weekend.
- Write to your grandchildren's favorite sports player, singer, or actor, and request an autographed picture for them.
- Share some memories with your grandchildren of how excited you and their parents were on the day they were born.
- Volunteer one day a week in a grandchild's classroom.
- Let your granddaughter polish her toenails and yours with a wild color.
- Make arrangements for you and your grandson to tour the local fire station or to attend a sporting event of his favorite team.
- Make or purchase matching pajamas for you, your grandchildren, and their favorite dolls or teddy bears.
- Always carry Band-Aids and gummy bears.
- Pray for your grandchildren every day. When you are together, make sure they hear you pray aloud for them.

*Children will remember you
not for the material things you provided
but for the feeling that you cherished them.*

Richard J. Evans

Through the Eyes of Love

Don Schmitz

A grandmother and her little grandson, whose face was sprinkled with bright freckles, were spending the day at the zoo. They saw lots of children waiting in line to get their faces painted. They decided they would get their faces painted too.

While standing in line, a little girl said to the freckled boy next to her, "You've got so many freckles, there's no place to paint on your face!"

Embarrassed, the little boy dropped his head and began to cry. His grandmother knelt down next to him. "I love your freckles! When I was a little girl, I always wanted freckles." She then took her finger and traced it around the child's cheek. "Freckles are beautiful."

The boy looked up. "Really?" he asked hesitantly.

"Of course," said the grandmother. "Why, just name one thing that's prettier than freckles."

The little boy thought for a moment, then peered directly into Grandmother's face and softly whispered, "Wrinkles."

Staying in Touch

If nothing is going well, call Grandmother!
Italian proverb

It's important to let your grandchildren know they are close to your heart no matter how many miles apart you are.

- Throughout the year, send your grandkids a disposable camera to take pictures for you of their family, friends, and pets. Compile an album of the photos to give as a keepsake gift one day.

- Technology is great, but getting "real" mail is like a hug from Grandma. Send cards on special days—and on ordinary days too. Decorate the envelopes with stickers, or draw borders of hearts, or put a lipstick kiss on the back.

- Put together care packages for occasions such as an illness, a good report card, or a home run. Enclose items as simple as a coloring book, stickers, a DVD, coupons for an ice cream parlor, or a small tin filled with coins.

- Record books on tape and send them to your grandchildren, along with a copy of each book. They will love hearing your voice read to them as they turn the pages of the book.

- Send e-mails and attach photos or links to games and other Web sites for grandkids to enjoy. Buy a Webcam for face-to-face chats, or use a chat feature so you can visit when you're both online.

- At Christmas, get someone to film you and Grandpa reading the Christmas story or singing "We Wish You a Merry Christmas." You can also film events like Grandpa winning a golf tournament.

- Younger grandkids love phone calls from grandparents. Call just to chat, sing a lullaby, or read a bedtime story to them.

- Ask your grandchildren for prayer requests. Let them know that you're always praying for them, even when you are apart.

- Schedule a standing weekly appointment or choose a special occasion to telephone your grandchildren at bedtime and sing a lullaby to them. End this special phone call by joining in their bedtime prayers with them.

Grandma's Book Club

For my grandchildren who live far away, I have a Grandma's Book Club. I send each one a monthly book and then call them to talk about the book. My grandchildren are young, but I hope to continue this as they grow in their maturity and love for reading.

Karen Robbins

*A garden of love
grows in a grandmother's heart.*

Author Unknown

Granny Camp

Martha Van Der Linden

One of the happiest memories of my childhood is Granny Camp," my eldest granddaughter, Jennifer, reminisced at a recent family wedding.

"Mine too," echoed her sisters, Stacey and Lindsey. As we rewound the mental videos of their annual visits to my house, the memories filled our hearts with joy.

Granny Camp was born out of my desire to provide a week or two of summer fun for my grandchildren. And, oh, the fun we had.

For years the girls and their brother, Kevin, and their cousins Tara and Erica came to Granny Camp. Now they were adults, and we laughed as we recalled the silly, ridiculous things we enjoyed back then—root-beer floats for breakfast, pancakes topped with strawberries sinking into mountains of whipped cream, and bedtimes so flexible we dared not mention the hour to their parents. While they nibbled forbidden junk food, I warned them, "Don't ever eat this stuff at home."

A favorite activity was fluffing up pillows on my bed as we snuggled up close to read their favorite books over and over again. We watched *Mary Poppins, The Sound of Music*, and *Beauty and the Beast* so often that the grandchildren learned the words to every song. Music, music, music! Grabbing an instrument from my sturdy basket, they would line up and march around the room, even out the door and down the street. Oh, how we giggled!

I felt a bit like Mary Poppins, snapping my fingers to make fun things happen—parks, pools, train rides, and picnics; carousel rides, children's theater, and Broadway shows. Dress-up was extra special. What wonderful dance routines and "show productions" my grandchildren put on!

Advancing from Candy Land to Monopoly, from wooden puzzles to five-hundred-piece ones, and from "The Itsy Bitsy Spider" to the music of their time, were all milestones. The years moved forward rapidly—all the way to the wedding, at which our Granny Camp reminiscing took place, and beyond—when Jennifer, who had become a mother herself, asked, "Can Jacob come to Granny Camp?"

Bright eyed and happy faced, my great-grandson Jacob arrived the next summer to enjoy all the silly things his mother had—and more. And so the tradition continues . . . another generation of grandchildren loving Granny Camp, coming to receive the precious gift of a grandmother's time.

Memory Book

When my grandchildren come for a visit, I give them a loose-leaf notebook with their photo and name on the cover. The notebook is filled with paper so they can record and illustrate the highlights of their visit. I transcribe for the younger children, but everyone draws pictures with markers and crayons. I keep copies of the children's books to savor. Their grandfather Pappi and I are amused to see our grandchildren's different perspectives on the same activity! Best of all, this has birthed a generation of excellent writers and artists in our family.

Peggy DiIorio

Hearts of Love

When you love somebody, your eyelashes go up and down and little stars come out of you.

Karen, age 7

When preschoolers at Hilltop Learning Center were asked how they knew their grandmothers loved them, their faces instantly lit up with smiles. They wiggled their toes, fluttered their eyelashes, and said things like "Because my grandma thanks God for me" . . . "She gives me hugs and kisses . . . plays with me . . . puts Band-Aids on my hurts." And, "She likes being with me!"

Since the heart is the universal symbol of love, Valentine's Day is a perfect time for grandmothers and grandchildren to celebrate together. Here are a few ideas that will give your grandkids more reasons to wiggle their toes and flutter their lashes when someone asks how they know their grandmothers love them.

Band-Aid Tattoos

Your younger grandchildren will think you're a really cool grandma when you surprise them with Band-Aid tattoos.

Use a paint pen or permanent marker to write *I Luv U* on sheer or flesh-toned Band-Aids. Decorate with small heart stickers, and make enough so each child can wear several. It will delight them all the more if Grandma wears one too.

Sharing Love

Let your grandchildren decorate a shoebox and fill it with homemade cookies. Deliver the cookies to a neighbor or family member who might need an extra touch of love on Valentine's Day.

Candy-Heart Bingo

Playing table games is always a hit with grandchildren, but imagine their absolute delight when you announce that you're going to play a game of Candy-Heart Bingo!

Use standard bingo cards, or create your own on the computer. Play just like regular bingo but use candy hearts for markers. Prizes can be small items like a fancy pencil, a sticker, a piece of wrapped candy, or a certificate for a three-minute back rub.

Lace Hearts

With a little bit of help from Grandmother, even a preschooler can make a lace heart. Cut pieces of florist wire (or any flexible wire) long enough to shape into the desired size heart. Next, cut a piece of lace eyelet twice as long as the wire. Show grandchildren how to weave the wire through the lace. Wrap the ends of the wire together and mold into a heart shape. Adjust the lace so the gathers are evenly distributed. Tie a delicate pink or red ribbon to the top. It's a perfect gift for grandchildren to give to someone they love—maybe even you!

You don't think you could possibly love
your grandchild more than you do today,
and then comes tomorrow.

Author Unknown

Teacups of Love

Nancy Jo Sullivan

When I was a little girl, every Sunday morning was like a holiday. After church, my family, all eleven of us, would gather in my grandmother's kitchen. Wrapped in the scents of warm cinnamon rolls and the sounds of small talk and percolating coffee, "Mema" would make her rounds, hugging us tightly, one by one, as if she hadn't seen us in years.

One Sunday morning, when I was nine years old, Mema's kitchen got a little crowded. I slipped away from the noisy congestion of family into Mema's dining room. It was a much quieter place, where warm sunlight streamed through paned picture windows and gilded rose prints adorned the walls.

Next to a drop-leaf table was a china hutch filled with polished teacups. During the hard years of the Great Depression, Mema had received each cup as a gift, a secondhand gift from a moneyless friend or relative.

"They're cups of love . . . priceless," Mema used to say.

That morning I found myself admiring the porcelain patterns of the keepsake cups: every petaled rose, each silver-edged heart, every etching of emerald ivy.

"Some day I'll collect teacups," I told myself as I pressed my hands against the glass doors of the hutch.

Mema peeked in on me from the kitchen. Drawing near, she saw me studying her collection.

"Which one do you like best?" she asked, smile wrinkles framing her cocoa brown eyes.

"That one!" I pointed to a sunlit cup; it was lavender, trimmed with strands of gold leaves.

Sixteen years later, on my wedding day, I opened a small package that Mema had wrapped with white foil paper. Underneath a lacy bow, she had tucked a card. *Your favorite*, it read. As I held the gift in my hand, I knew it would be the first teacup in my collection.

The early years of my marriage passed quickly. My husband and I didn't have much money, but I could always find a few dollars for the teacups hidden by the chipped punch bowls at garage sales.

Gradually I filled each shelf of an old glass-doored cabinet with secondhand teacups. I placed Mema's wedding-gift cup in the middle of the collection—it would always remain my favorite.

But while I was busy adding cups to my hutch, Mema was giving hers away. She was growing older and weaker, cancer invading her bones; nonetheless, she made sure her keepsake cups found a home.

Mema's health began to worsen, and I visited her one last time. Before I reached the bedroom where she lay, I passed through her dining room. Stopping for a moment, I pressed my hands against the glass doors of the hutch and peered inside. All of the cups were gone; only lines of sunlight filled the shelves.

Moments later, I sat at her bedside.

"Mema," I whispered. "Your teacups . . . were they hard to give away?"

Mema took my hand. Though her breathing was labored, her eyes were warm and brown and bright.

"They were cups of love . . . and love is meant to be shared," she replied. As Mema drifted off to sleep, I closed my eyes with a clear and lovely image.

Mema's life was like a beautifully patterned teacup, brimming with a lifetime of unforgettable tenderness, given to our family as a gift.

She was like a "keepsake" passed down to us from God, ours to cherish deeply, ours to admire forever in the "hutches" of our hearts.

Tender Moments

As your grandchildren grow from babies to adulthood, you will experience many tender moments along the way. Some of the most precious come when you're teaching young hearts to comprehend God's great love. The faith you share with them will provide a lifetime of joy as well as strength to withstand life's sorrows.

- Sing songs of faith as you rock your grandchildren to sleep.
- Kneel with them by their beds to say nighttime prayers.
- Make it a point to say blessings around the table and read often from a favorite Bible storybook.
- Teach them to give their time and resources to help others.
- Sit outside under the stars and tell them the wonderful creation story.

*A*nother way to help little ones understand the Christian faith is by making a wordless book together. Time and time again they will pick it up and say, "Tell me again, Grandma—tell me about the greatest story ever told."

As its name implies, there are no words in this book—only paper of five different colors to represent the central parts of the gospel message. Cut five pieces of colored card stock to the size you want.

- Black—for sin that separates us from God (Romans 3:23)
- Red—for the death of Jesus on the cross (John 3:16)
- White—for God's forgiveness of our sins (1 John 1:9)
- Green—for spiritual growth (Colossians 1:10)
- Gold—for eternity in heaven (John 14:1–3)

Punch holes on one side of each card, and tie the pages together with ribbon. Then snuggle up together to share the truth that can make such a difference in your grandchildren's lives.

Jesus said, "Let the little children come to me."

Matthew 19:14 NIV

Acknowledgments

Formal Permissions

"Dear Heart" from *Grandmother by Another Name* by Carolyn J. Booth and Mindy B. Henderson, Rutledge Hill Press, Nashville, TN, © 1997, p. 42. Reprinted with permission.

"Show and Tell" by Lois Wyse in her book *Funny, You Don't Look Like a Grandmother*, Crown Publishing Group, New York, NY, © 1988. Reprinted with permission.

"Dinner Out" by Maryann Lee Jacob, © 1997. Reprinted with permission from the author. All rights reserved.

"A Bride Doll" by Shirley Rose, © 2006. Reprinted with permission from Jerry and Shirley Rose, authors of *GPS: God's Plan for Significance*, SigLiv Publishers, Aurora, IL, © 2006.

"Learned by Heart" author unknown. This story is quoted in various versions on the Internet. It is also quoted in several books, including *I Shall Not Want* by Robert T. Ketchum, Moody Publishing, Chicago, IL, © 1953.

"Through the Eyes of Love" by Don Schmitz, author of *The New Face of Grandparenting* and the founder of The Grandkidsandme Foundation, www.grandkidsandme.org. Reprinted with permission of the author.

"Granny Camp" by Martha Van Der Linden, © 2006. Reprinted with permission of the author.

"Teacups of Love" from *Moments of Grace* by Nancy Jo Sullivan, © 2000, Multnomah Publishers, Inc., Sisters, OR. Condensed and reprinted with permission of the author.

General Acknowledgments

We wish to thank the following women who allowed us to reprint the charming ideas and treasured memories that are sprinkled throughout this book: Diane Van Wyk, Mary Ellen Hansen, Karen Robbins, Grandmother

Benefield, Margaret "Mock-Mock" Westerman, Mimi Huey, Sally Knower, Karen Ellison, Patty Duncan, Pamela Brown, Kimber Annie Engstrom, and Peggy DiIorio.

We've adapted some items in this book from snippets and ideas we've gathered through the years from family, friends, churches, schools, magazines, and books. Recent discoveries were adapted from the following sources: Ice Ball Surprise and Living Easter Basket from www.amazingmoms.com; Five-Fingered Prayer, author unknown, from *Lists to Live By: The Christian Collection*, Multnomah Publishers, Sisters, OR, © 2004; Ways to Love Your Grandchildren, items 2 and 6 from *The I Love You Book, More than 500 Ways to Show the Ones You Love that You Care*, by Cynthia MacGregor and Vic Bobb, Conari Press, Berkeley, CA, © 2002; Staying in Touch, item 1, from *Long Distance Grandma* by Janet Teitsort, published by Howard Books, West Monroe, Louisiana, © 2005; Candy-Heart Bingo from www.theideabox.com.